THE FLUTE

THE FLUTE

An Illustrated
Step-by-Step
Instructional Guide

Frank Cappelli

ELDORADO INK

Eldorado Ink
PO Box 100097
Pittsburgh, PA 15233
www.eldoradoink.com

First printing

1 3 5 7 9 8 6 4 2

Library of Congress Cataloging-in-Publication Data

Cappelli, Frank.
  The flute / Frank Cappelli.
     p. cm. — (Learn to play)
  Includes bibliographical references (p.   ) and index.
  ISBN-13: 978-1-932904-13-0
  ISBN-10: 1-932904-13-1
  1. Flute—Methods. I. Title.
  MT342.C19 2007
  788.3'2193—dc22

                                    2006036437

Acknowledgements

The author would like to thank all of those who provided instruments to
be used in the photographs of this book, particularly Volkwein's Music
of Pittsburgh (800-553-8742; www.volkweins.com).

TABLE OF CONTENTS

Introduction   9

Part One: Getting Started
    1. Buying a Flute   10
    2. Assembling the Flute   12
    3. Cleaning the Flute   15

Part Two: Reading Music
    1. The Staff   16
    2. The Notes   17
    3. Reading Musical Notes   19
    4. Clef Symbols   20
    5. Time Signature   20
    6. The Sharp and Flat Signs   21
    7. Breathing Marks   23

Part Three: Getting Ready to Play
    1. Breathing   24
    2. Making a Sound   24
    3. Holding the Flute   25

4. Your First Note (F)   29

5. F Exercises   30

6. Playing the Note G   33

7. G Exercises   33

8. F and G Exercises   36

Part Four: Let's Play!

1. The Note A   40

2. A Exercises   41

3. Playing What You Know: F, G, and A   43

4. The Note Bb   45

5. Bb Exercises   45

6. The Note B   48

7. B Exercises   48

8. The Note Upper C   51

9. Upper C Exercises   51

10. Practicing What You Know: F Through Upper C   54

11. The Note Upper D   57

12. Upper D Exercises   57

13. The Note Upper Eb   60

14. Upper Eb Exercises   60

15. The Note Upper E   63

16. Upper E Exercises   63

17. The Note Upper F   68

18. Upper F Exercises   68

19. F Scales and New Songs   71

20. The Note Upper G   76

21. Upper G Exercises   76

22. The Note Upper A   82

23. Upper A Exercises   82

24. The F Scale   85
25. The Note E   86
26. E Exercises   86
27. Playing the Notes You Know   89
28. The Note Upper B   94
29. Upper B Exercises   94
30. The Note High C   97
31. High C Exercises   97

Appendix: Finding the Notes   102
Flute Timeline   104
Internet Resources   106
Glossary   108
Index   111
About the Author   112

Learn to Play

Clarinet
Flute
Guitar
Piano
Trumpet
Violin

INTRODUCTION

In many ways, the flute is a unique and unusual instrument. It is considered part of the woodwind family, even though for the past two centuries nearly all flutes have been made of metals. (Flutes used by professionals are usually made from pure silver, or sometimes other metals like gold or platinum; flutes for beginners are often made of brass with silver plating.) Most woodwinds need a reed to play, but the flute does not. And unlike other wind instruments, you do not blow into the flute; you blow across it. In fact, the word *flute* comes from the Latin word *flare,* which means "to flow"—a reference, perhaps, to the flowing stream of air required to play the instrument.

The flute is popular because its tones blend easily with other instruments. The sound of the flute is truly magical—it can be high and penetrating or low and spooky. More than any other instrument, perhaps, the flute has been associated with magic and witchcraft. In Mozart's 1791 opera *The Magic Flute,* the main character (Tamino) is given a flute that can be used to change men's minds. This power saves his life during the opera.

People have been playing flutelike instruments for thousands of years. It is impossible to say where or when the first flute was developed, but scholars know that the ancient Chinese made the instruments from bamboo, wood, and sometimes bone. Flutes have appeared in many other cultures, and have taken many forms throughout history.

In medieval Europe a flutelike instrument called a fife became a regular part of military bands. The sound was loud and shrill, carrying a good distance. Like most flutes of the time, the fife had only six holes and a limited range. This design was dominant until the mid-19th century, when Theobald Boehm designed a flute that became the model for the modern instrument. He added more holes and fashioned a system of keys to stop and unstop those additional holes, making it possible for a flutist to play a much broader range of notes than ever before.

This book presents a fresh approach to learning the flute, which will enable you to learn how to play and enjoy this wonderful instrument. Whether you are a true beginner, have a bit of musical training, or are a skilled musician on another instrument, the carefully developed approach of this book can help anyone succeed.

PART ONE: Getting Started

This book is intended for the beginning flute player. Anyone can play the flute; as with most other things in life, the level of success you will achieve depends on how much time you want to put into learning how to play.

To become a good flute player (a flutist or flautist), you need to work hard and practice. Give yourself time and always look for new ways to make yourself better. One way to do this is to listen to your favorite songs and see whether you can pick out notes or melodies that you can play on your own. Even if you can't play the entire song at first, this kind of practicing will improve your skill. Also, play with other musicians whenever you get the chance. You will learn from them as they will learn from you.

You will experience exhilaration and frustration as you learn to understand and master the flute. Hopefully the way this book is structured will make your experience as stress-free as possible. The instructions, diagrams, and illustrations will help you through everything from the purchase of a flute to playing your first songs.

1. Buying a Flute

Any time you plan to purchase a musical instrument, it is worthwhile to go to one or more music stores. This gives you an opportunity to ask questions and try out different instruments. Most people who work in a good music store are musicians and will be happy to talk about music. If you're looking for a flute, ask for someone who specializes in woodwinds.

If you decide to buy a flute, the price will probably be about $100 to $400, depending on the model. Beginner flutes are commonly silver-plated. More

expensive flutes are made from solid silver, so it makes sense for beginners to avoid this expense until they are certain they want to play the flute. Yamaha and Conn-Selmer are two good brands for beginners. However, every flute has its own sound, so try several different models if you can. If you are working with a flute teacher, or have a friend who has experience playing the flute, ask that person to come to the store with you. He or she will be able to judge the sound of the instrument a bit better than you could.

In addition to listening to the sound, make sure that the keys work smoothly and that the pads fit correctly. Check the head and body joint for warping and make sure the tube is straight, smooth, and does not have any dents.

HELPFUL TIP:
When looking for your first flute, it may be wise to rent an instrument. Renting allows you to try out the flute and even compare different flutes before you commit to a certain brand or model.

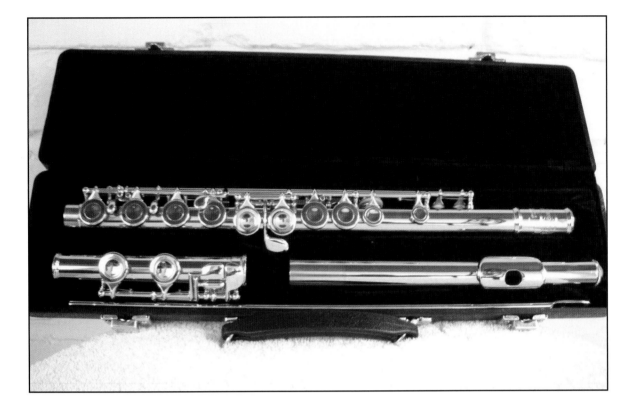

2. Assembling the Flute

The flute is a delicate instrument and needs to be treated with care. Even though you have only three pieces to put together, your instrument is made up of more than 150 pillars, rods, keys, rollers, and springs. If any of them are damaged, it will affect the sound of your flute.

To start with, place the instrument case on a flat surface and make sure the latches are facing you. When you open the lid, you will see the three pieces of the flute. These are the head joint, the body joint, and the foot joint.

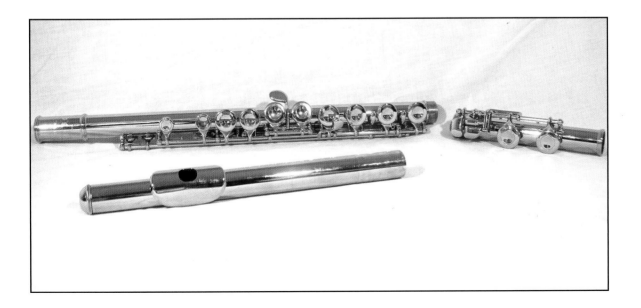

The Head Joint: The head joint (pictured above) has no keys. Instead you will find the lip plate, or the embouchure plate, where you place your lower lip. The blow hole, where air enters the flute, is located on the top of the lip plate. A smaller blow hole helps a professional flutist in playing the higher notes, while a larger hole helps in playing lower notes.

The Body Joint: The body joint (shown below) is the largest piece and has the most keys and pads.

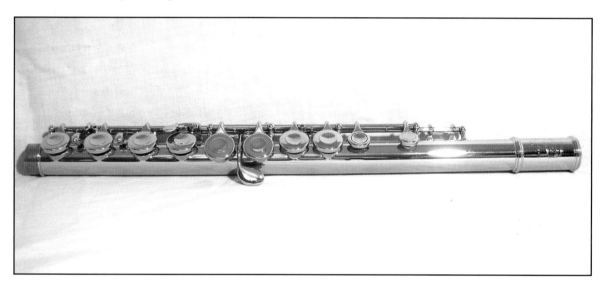

The Foot Joint: The foot joint is the shortest piece and has only a few keys. It is important to know that the rod on the foot joint does not line up with the rod on the body joint when you go to assemble the pieces.

As you take the pieces out, be careful. Try not to squeeze the key pads too tightly when putting the pieces together as the key pads will wear out faster. A beginner's flute is fairly sturdy, so as long as you don't abuse it, it should stand up to normal handling.

Pick up the head joint first, then the body joint. Hold the head joint in your left hand and the body joint in your right hand. With a twisting motion, connect the two parts. To line up the head joint with the body joint, look down the flute from the lip plate and line up the blow hole with the second keypad on the body joint. Be sure you are looking at the second key.

To attach the foot joint, hold the barrel of the flute in one hand and put the foot joint in the palm of your other hand. Line up the foot joint and the body joint by following the pipe along the side of the body joint. The pipe on the foot joint should not line up with the pipe of the body joint. The pipe along the foot joint has a ball at the end that should line up with the front edge of the third finger key on the body joint. The flute will sound the same regardless of where the keys are; the aim here is being able to reach all the keys comfortably.

When you are ready to take the flute apart, gently twist the joints with a pulling motion. If the joints start to stick or become difficult to twist, a small amount of instrument wax may be applied.

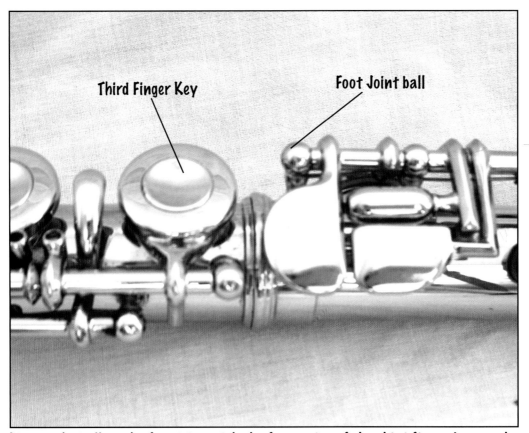

Line up the ball on the foot joint with the front edge of the third finger key on the body joint.

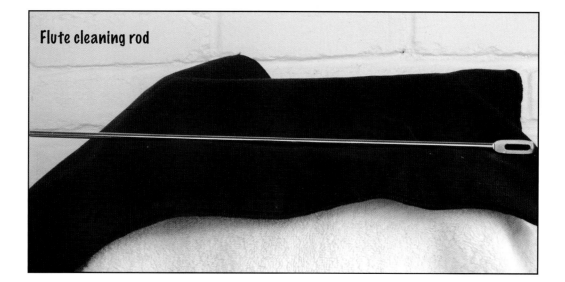

Flute cleaning rod

3. Cleaning the Flute

Before you put your flute away, you must clean it. To do this, you'll want to carry a cleaning rod and a clean handkerchief or clean cloth in your case. The cleaning rod can be made of wood or metal. At one end of the cleaning rod is an opening for the handkerchief or small cloth. Take a corner of the handkerchief or cloth and put it through the opening of the rod. Pull it through about a quarter of the way and fold the larger part over the rod to cover the entire rod with the cloth.

To clean the head joint, carefully insert the cloth and rod until it stops. Do not push too hard because if the metal on the inside is dented or damaged the quality of the sound will change.

Pick up each remaining piece of the flute by the barrel and slide the rod through. Do this very carefully so you do not damage the bottoms of the keypads. One time through is usually enough. Once this is done, take the same cloth and carefully wipe your fingerprints off the flute. If necessary, you can carefully place a finger in the tube to help steady the flute as you clean.

When you clean the tops of the body and foot joint keys, do not use a circular motion; instead, wipe them straight across. Place each piece back into the case once you have finished cleaning it.

Try not to leave your flute out of the case when you are not playing, as it could get dented or damaged. Also, do not leave a damp cloth in the case with the flute. Remember to clean your flute often. If you follow these simple instructions, your flute will last a long time.

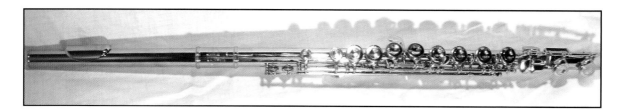

PART TWO: Reading Music

With what you will learn in this section, you will be able to communicate with musicians all around the world. I'll make it as painless as possible, but you've got to put in some time.

1. The Staff

The following will introduce you to some very basic concepts that will help you understand the notes on the flute. First, music is a language, and it is written on a staff. A staff has five lines and four spaces.

The lines and spaces are named starting at the bottom and going up, as illustrated by the staff below.

To give order to the music, the staff is divided into measures. A vertical line called a bar is used to mark out the measures. You know you're at the end of a section of music when you see a double bar line on the staff. Here is the staff with a G clef (also called a treble clef) with a 4/4 time signature and double bar line.

The double bar line tells a musician that he or she is at the end of a section or strain of music. Sometimes, however, there will be two dots before the double bar line. That means to repeat the section of music.

One other thing you may see when you are reading music is a small number at the beginning of some measures (circled in red below). This is just a helpful guide for the musician; it lets you know what measure you are playing. This can be particularly useful when you are playing music with a group and the leader or instructor wants you to start at a particular measure, rather than at the beginning of the song. Although in this book the number appears above the staff at the first measure of each line of music, in other music you may find that the number appears at the bottom of the staff, or that each measure is numbered.

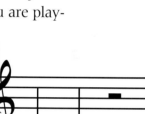

Repeat Sign

2. The Notes

Next we shall take a look at what gets written on the staff. The notes tell us what tones to play, and take on the names of the lines or spaces they occupy. A note has three parts.

The Head: gives a general indication of time: a hollow oval indicates a half note or a whole note, while a solid oval denotes a quarter, eighth, or other note.

The Head

The Stem: all notes except for whole notes have a stem.

The Stem

The Flag: the presence of a flag indicates an eighth or sixteenth note.

The Flag

You can find notes *on* the staff, *above* the staff, and *below* the staff.

Quarter Note

Half Note

Eighth Note

Whole Note

A quarter note has a stem and a solid oval head. It usually gets one count. If there are four beats in the measure, you might count "one, two, three, four" in your mind when playing; the quarter note would generally be played for the amount of time it takes to count "one."

Notes with a stem and hollow oval head are called half notes. A half note gets two counts, or beats, per measure. It is twice as long as a quarter note, so count "one, two."

An eighth note has a solid head, a stem, and a flag. Often, two eighth notes will be connected. The eighth note lasts half as long as a quarter note. So if you are mentally counting the beats in the measure, you would count "one and two and three and four and." Each of these words would represent an eighth note; you would play one eighth note on the "one" and a second on the "and."

A whole note is a hollow circle. It indicates a note that receives four beats.

Sometimes, you will see a dot next to a note, as shown in the lower left corner. This means that when you play the note, you need to add one-half the original value of the note to its length. For example, a dotted half note is played for three beats, while a dotted quarter note is extended by an extra eighth. (In 4/4 time each measure would have eight eighth notes; the dotted quarter note would be played for three eighths.)

Rests also appear in the measure. These symbols indicate to the musician when he or she should take a brief break from playing. Like notes, there are different symbols for rests, depending on how long the musician should be silent. Two common rests, quarter note and half note rests, are pictured below.

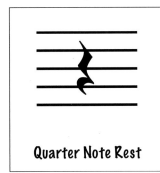

Dotted Half Note

Quarter Note Rest

Half Note Rest

3. Reading Musical Notes

Now that you have been introduced to reading music, it's time to take the next step. You have seen the staff, with its five lines and four spaces. You now need to learn the names of the lines and spaces of the staff. Here are the notes on the lines:

The note on the bottom line is E. The next line up is G, then B, then D, and finally F. Most students use a mnemonic device to remember the lines. They memorize the phrase:

Every **G**ood **B**oy **D**eserves **F**udge

The spaces from the bottom up are F, A, C, E. Yes, it's the word "face," which is another mnemonic that students can use to remember the notes in the spaces.

Music uses only the letters A through G, and the notes are always in alphabetical order. So if you start on the bottom line, E, the next space is F, the next line is G, and the following space is A. The next line will be B and so on. However, notes can also be written above and below the staff:

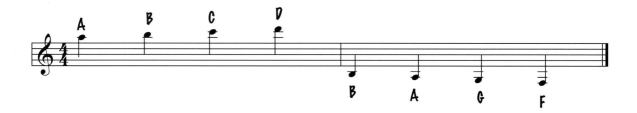

In the example above, some of the notes have an extra line or two through them, either above or below the five-line staff. These are called ledger lines, and they help the musician to easily identify the proper note.

4. Clef Symbols

In the previous section, specific notes were assigned to the lines and spaces on the staff. The way that you can be sure what note each line or space represents is to look at the beginning of the first staff of music. There, you will see a symbol called a clef. There are several different clef symbols; each indicates to the person reading the music which notes the lines and spaces on the staff represent. For the flute you will only need to know one, the treble, or G, clef. When you see the treble clef, you'll know that the notes on the lines are EGBDF and the notes on the spaces are FACE.

The Treble Clef

Another commonly used clef is the bass clef, but this is mostly found in piano and bass instrument music. While we won't be covering how to read bass clef in this book, it's still good to know the symbol in case you ever come across it. The lines and spaces in bass clef have different note values than the lines and spaces in treble clef.

The Bass Clef

5. Time Signature

In addition to the clef, there is also a time signature written at the beginning of the musical staff. The time signature tells the musician how many beats are in each measure and which note is valued at one beat.

The top number indicates the number of beats per measure. So in 4/4 time, there are four beats per measure, while in 3/4 time there are three beats per measure. The bottom number tells which note gets one beat. A 4 on the bottom of the time signature means the quarter note gets one beat. In 6/8 time each measure would have 6 beats and the eighth note would be played as one beat.

Let's Review

1. Music is written on a **staff**, which has **five** lines and **four** spaces.
2. The notes of the lines are **EGBDF.**
3. The notes of the spaces are **FACE.**
4. Flute music is normally written in the **treble clef.**
5. The staff is divided into **measures** by vertical lines called **bar lines.**

Below are some examples of time signatures that are often used in flute music. You will sometimes see a C in the place of a time signature. That simply stands for 4/4, or common time. Most of the music you will see will be written either in 4/4 or 3/4 time.

2/4 Time   4/4 Time
(also known as common time)

3/4 Time   6/8 Time

6. The Sharp and Flat Signs

The figure on the F line on the staff to the right is called a sharp. If you see it placed in front of a note, you should play the note a half step up. For example, if you see an F with the # before it, you would not play F, you would play the note a half tone higher. This note is called F#.

Notes can also be flat, which means they are played a half tone lower. A flat sign looks like a small b (pictured at left). As you've probably figured out, sharps and flats can indicate the same tone. The note G is one step above F, so you use the same fingering to play F# (a half-step up) and Gb (a half-step down). These are known as enharmonic notes.

The first place you will see flats and sharps is in the key signature. If you see one sharp in the key signature (like in the first image in this section) the music is in the key of G. If you see one flat in the key signature (as in the second image in this section), the music is in the key of F. At the top of the next page are the sharps and flats that will appear in the key signatures of some other musical keys.

The Key of D   The Key of A   The Key of E   The Key of B

The Key of Bb   The Key of Eb   The Key of Ab   The Key of C

Sometimes a song may include a note or notes that are not in the same key as the rest of the song. When this happens, you will see a sharp or flat symbol next to the note in your music. If the note is already sharp or flat, you may see another symbol next to the note. This means to play the natural tone. Musicians call these notes "accidentals."

Natural Symbol

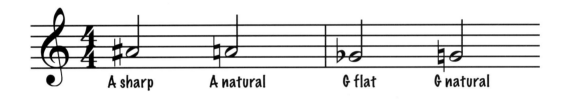

A sharp   A natural   G flat   G natural

7. Breathing Marks

When reading music written for the flute (as well as some other wind instruments), you may see small marks that look like apostrophes, as shown below.

These are known as breathing marks, and they tell you when to take a breath so that you'll be prepared to play the next measure. Breathing marks are not rests, however, so be sure to draw in a breath quickly. If you take too long, you won't be able to play the next note on the proper beat.

Some songs do not have breathing marks because the music has rests that are spaced in such a way that the musician can take a break when needed. If the music you're looking at has no breathing marks, you should take a breath whenever you come to a rest.

PART THREE: Getting Ready to Play

1. Breathing

The flute is a wind instrument, and the most important thing to learn in order to play is how to breathe correctly. Practicing your breathing will allow you to play longer without becoming exhausted; it will also help you to play longer notes.

Posture is important. You should stand tall with your head up and your neck and shoulders relaxed. Your weight should be equally balanced on both feet. If you are sitting, use the same posture, but sit at the front of the chair.

Imagine someone coming toward you and suddenly thrusting a finger toward your bellybutton. Your reaction would be to quickly draw in your stomach. The area that you sucked in is called your diaphragm, and those are the muscles you must use to control your breathing.

Slowly breathe in and fill that area below your stomach with air. Don't lift your shoulders, just expand your diaphragm and then slowly let the air out. As you do this, practice controlling the flow of air. Always breathe in through your nose and out through your mouth.

2. Making a Sound

At some time in your life you've probably blown across the top of an empty bottle to make a sound. This is very similar to the way a flute is played. Hold the opening of the lip plate against your lips and rotate it forward so that the opening is facing up, approximately horizontal. Place the head joint in the curve of your chin so the embouchure plate rests just below your lower lip. The bottom edge of your lower lip should feel the inside edge of the blow hole. Your bottom lip should cover about one-third of the embouchure hole. Form your lips like you would say the letter "M." Using the sound "pu," blow a stream of air. For a shorter tone place the tip of your tongue on the gum line just behind your top teeth, and whisper the word "too" as you blow.

You may need to experiment by adjusting the flute forward or backward slightly to achieve a clear and clean tone. Don't get discouraged; you can do it, even though it may take some time at first. Remember, learning any instrument involves a lot of practice.

You can practice the proper breathing techniques without holding your flute by just using the head joint. This will also help you to develop your embouchure, the muscles in your face that are needed to play the flute. To do this, hold the closed end of the head joint with your left hand, cover the other end with the palm of your right hand, and bring the head joint into playing position.

When you are first starting out, make sure that you limit the amount of time that you practice or play. If you begin to get dizzy or if your arms, wrists, or fingers start to tingle, stop playing for a while. You might be trying to blow too hard, which will strain your muscles and can also make you feel light-headed.

3. Holding the Flute

With the flute assembled, bring the flute up to your mouth. Your left elbow should be in front of you, pointing down and to the left of center. It should line up with your left foot. Your left hand should be facing you with the flute resting on the base of your left index finger near the mouthpiece. Your wrist should be slightly bent, and your thumb should wrap underneath the flute. Your right hand should be toward the foot of the flute, facing away from you. Your right thumb is placed under the flute to balance it. Your right elbow should be pointing down and to the right of your body. The end of your flute should angle slightly down and forward.

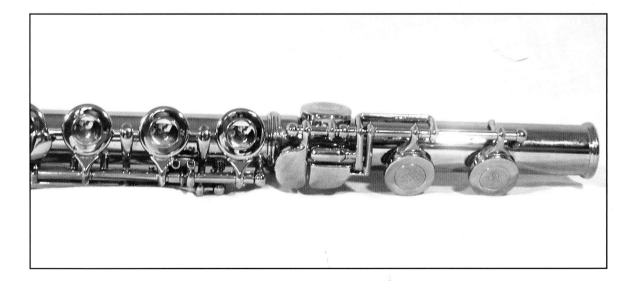

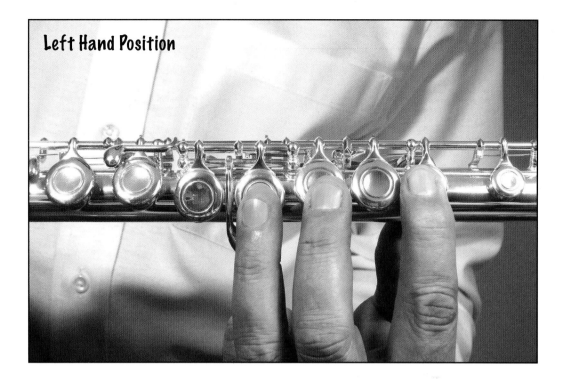

Left Hand Position

Rest your left thumb on the long straight key on the back side of the middle joint. Place the first, second, and third fingers of your left hand on the second, fourth and fifth keys of the middle joint. Curve your fingers so the finger pads are above the center of the keys.

Your right hand should face away from you. Curve your first three fingers above the last three keys of the middle joint. Your right wrist should be arched a bit but relaxed. The pinky should rest naturally on side keys without pressing them. The thumb is placed under the flute to help with support and to help keep your fingers in the correct positions. Your arms should be up, relaxed, and away from your body.

As you learn notes and practice the exercises and songs in this book, you'll see references to various fingers. For both your left and right hands,

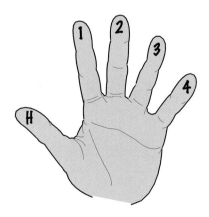

Left hand fingering

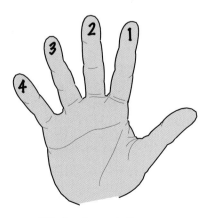

Right hand fingering

Right Hand Position

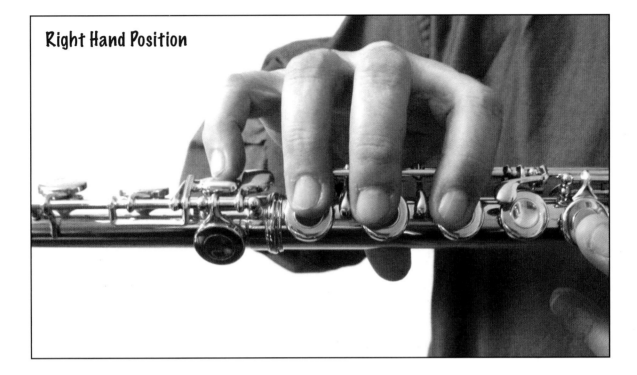

your index finger will be referred to as your 1 finger, your middle finger is the 2 finger, your ring finger is the 3 finger, and your pinky is the 4 finger. Sometimes you'll use your left thumb to play notes; it is labeled H.

All fingers should be gently curved and placed over the appropriate keys. It takes practice to hold the flute without depressing any keys.

Although the flute seems like a light instrument, when you begin playing your fingers will become tired from holding the instrument. When this happens, take a break. It won't be long before you are able to play for hours at a time, so don't become discouraged if you are only able to hold the instrument for a short time at first.

HELPFUL TIP:
The thumb of your left hand is the only thumb that plays a key. If you see notation that calls for the thumb to play, it always means the left thumb.

Parts of the Flute

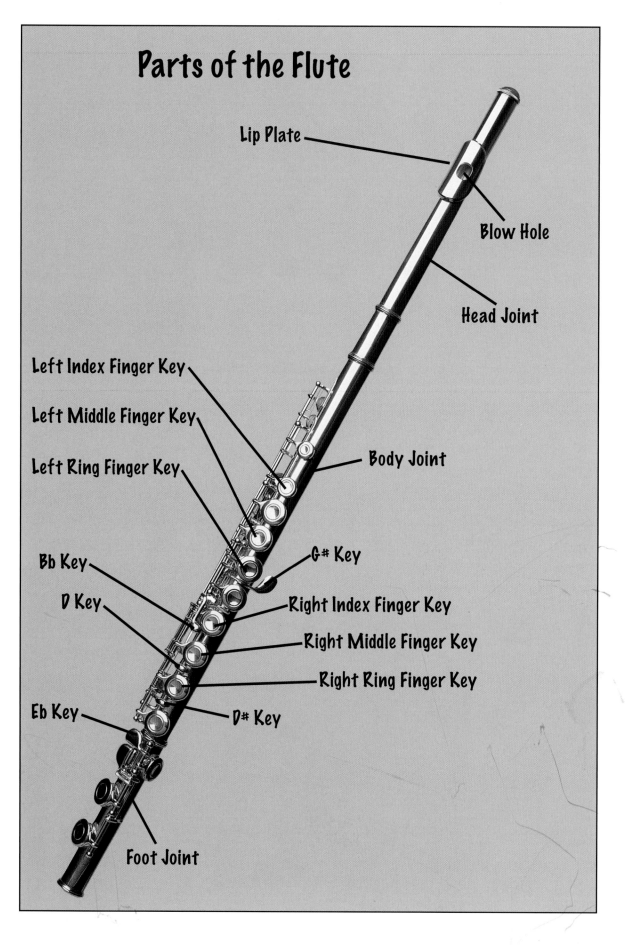

Lip Plate

Blow Hole

Head Joint

Left Index Finger Key

Left Middle Finger Key

Left Ring Finger Key

Body Joint

Bb Key

G# Key

D Key

Right Index Finger Key

Right Middle Finger Key

Right Ring Finger Key

Eb Key

D# Key

Foot Joint

4. Your First Note (F)

Because this is a book intended for beginners, we will take a simplified approach to identifying the notes that you are learning. For a more advanced explanation and the proper names for the notes, please see the Appendix.

The first note that you will learn to play is the note F. To play it, close the keys underneath your left thumb and the first three fingers of your left hand. Close the keys underneath the first finger of your right hand and the first key on the foot joint with your right little finger. The other fingers should rest in their positions and not press any keys.

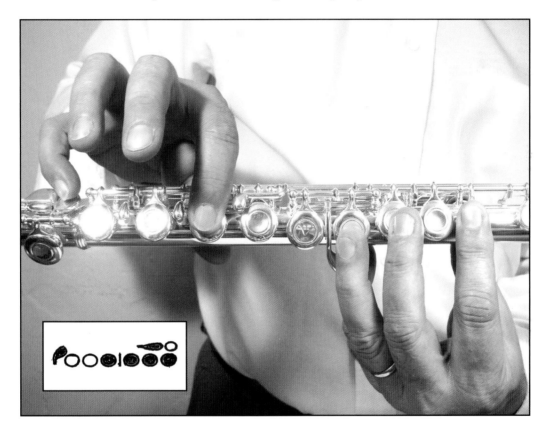

Remember to whisper "too" as you begin each note. Use a nice strong flow of air.

Here is the note F in music. The note as written here is a half note, meaning that it would be played for two of the four beats.

On the next few pages are some simple exercises that will help you practice playing the note F. It is not important to play them fast; instead, focus on playing the note clearly and cleanly.

5. F Exercises

Practice playing F with these simple exercises. In the first exercise, you will play half notes. Here, since the music is in 4/4 time, the half note is played for two beats. You'll play the note on beats one and two and rest on three and four.

F, half notes, exercise 1

In the quarter note exercise below, you'll play the F only on the first and second beats of each measure.

F, quarter notes, exercise 1

When playing whole notes in 4/4 time, the note is held for four beats.

F, whole notes, exercise 1

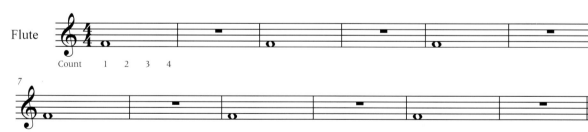

Play four eighth notes in the first two beats of each measure ("one-and-two-and"), and rest on the last two beats.

F, eighth notes, exercise 1

Use the following exercises to improve both your skill at producing a note clearly and your ability to recognize different types of notes.

F, half notes, exercise 2

F, quarter notes, exercise 2

F, whole notes, exercise 2

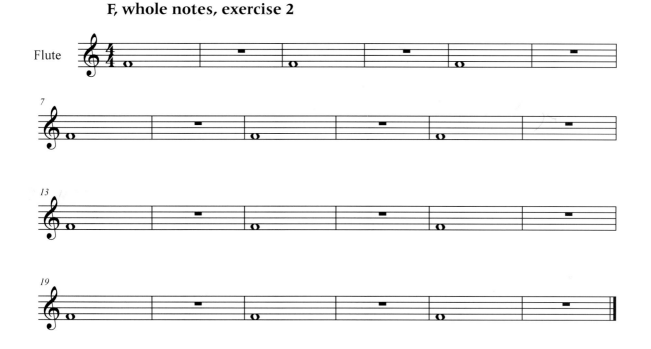

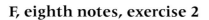

F, eighth notes, exercise 2

6. Playing the Note G

The second note you need to learn is the note G. To play this note, close the keys underneath your left thumb and the three fingers on your left hand. Close only the key on the foot joint with your right little finger.

The Note G

7. G Exercises

Use the following exercises to practice playing G.

G, half notes, exercise 1

G, quarter notes, exercise 1

G, whole notes, exercise 1

G, eighth notes, exercise 1

G, half notes, exercise 2

G, quarter notes, exercise 2

G, whole notes, exercise 2

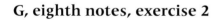

G, eighth notes, exercise 2

8. F and G Exercises

Now try switching between both of the notes you have learned. You'll only be shifting the index finger of your right hand to do this.

F and G, half notes, exercise 1

F and G, quarter notes, exercise 1

F and G, whole notes, exercise 1

F and G, eighth notes, exercise 1

F and G, half notes, exercise 2

F and G, quarter notes, exercise 2

This Japanese print from around 1860 shows a woman playing a flute.

F and G, whole notes, exercise 2

F and G, eighth notes, exercise 2

Did You Know?

Leonardo da Vinci, George Washington, Czar Nicholas II of Russia, and Henry David Thoreau are all known to have played the flute.

PART FOUR:

Let's Play!

Now that you have gotten the feel for your flute and practiced playing some simple but important notes, you're ready to learn the other notes that you will need to know in order to play songs.

1. The Note A

To play the note A, close the keys underneath your left thumb and the first and second fingers on your left hand. Close only the key on the foot joint with your right little finger.

The Note A

2. A Exercises

Here are some exercises you can use to practice playing the note A.

A, half notes, exercise 1

A, quarter notes, exercise 1

A, whole notes, exercise 1

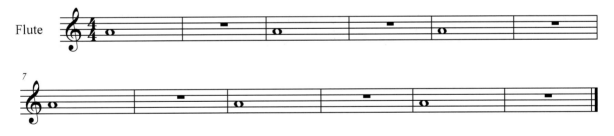

A, eighth notes, exercise 1

A, half notes, exercise 2

A, quarter notes, exercise 2

A, eighth notes, exercise 2

3. Playing What You Know: F, G, and A

With the following exercises, you'll practice switching between the notes F, G, and A.

F, G, and A, half notes, exercise 1

F, G, and A, quarter notes, exercise 1

F, G, and A, whole notes, exercise 1

F, G, and A, eighth notes, exercise 1

F, G, and A, half notes, exercise 2

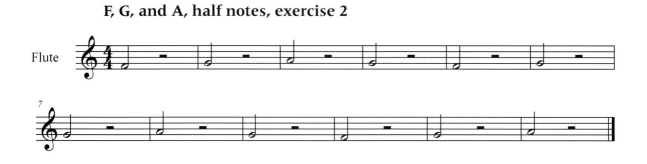

F, G, and A, quarter notes, exercise 2

F, G, and A, whole notes, exercise 2

F, G, and A, eighth notes, exercise 2

4. The Note Bb

Now let's try playing the note Bb. Close the keys underneath your left thumb and the first key with your index finger. Close the first key with your right index finger and the foot joint key with your right little finger.

The Note Bb

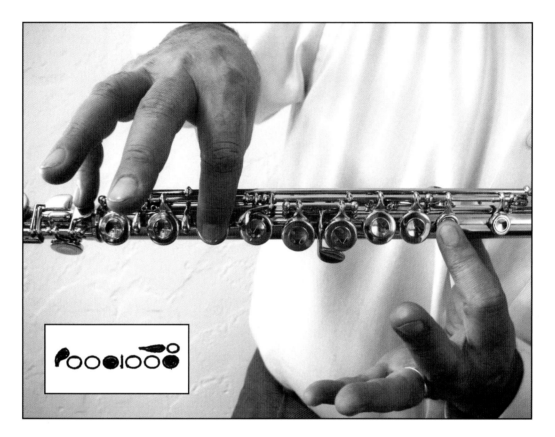

5. Bb Exercises

Here are some exercises you can use to practice playing the note Bb.

Bb, half notes, exercise 1

Remember, once the flat sign appears before a note in a measure, that note must be played flat for the rest of the measure, unless you see a natural sign before the note.

Bb, quarter notes, exercise 1

Bb, whole notes, exercise 1

Bb, eighth notes, exercise 1

Bb, half notes, exercise 2

Bb, quarter notes, exercise 2

Bb, whole notes, exercise 2

Bb, eighth notes, exercise 2

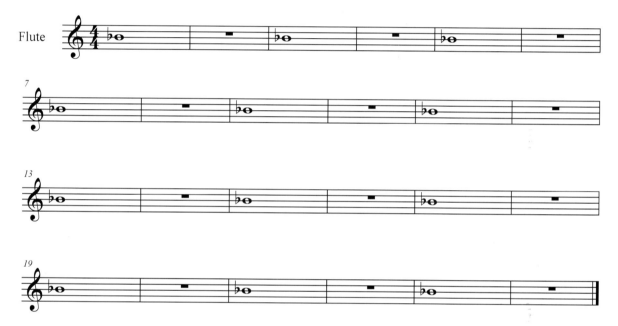

6. The Note B

To play a B, make a slight alteration to the Bb. Close the keys underneath your left thumb and the first key with your index finger on your left hand. But now only close the foot joint key with your right little finger.

The Note B

7. B Exercises

Here are some exercises you can use to practice playing the note B.

B, half notes, exercise 1

B, quarter notes, exercise 1

B, whole notes, exercise 1

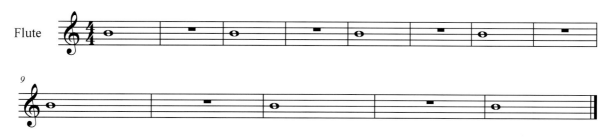

B, eighth notes, exercise 1

B, half notes, exercise 2

B, quarter notes, exercise 2

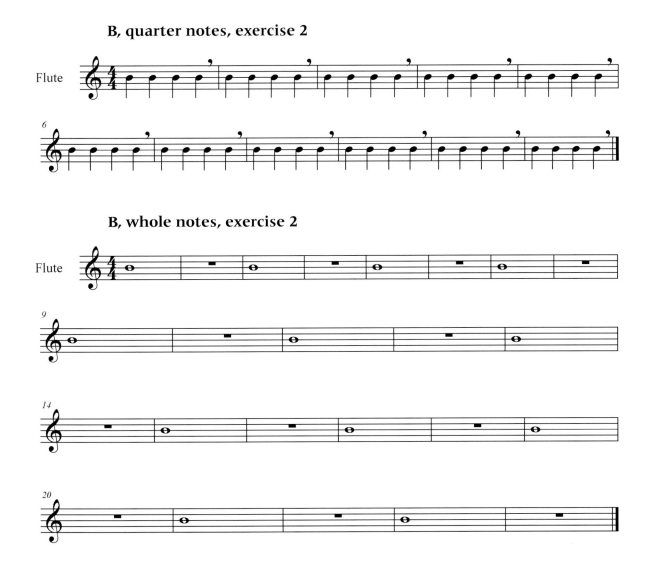

B, whole notes, exercise 2

B, eighth notes, exercise 2

8. The Note Upper C

To play this note, just close the first key with the index finger of your left hand and the foot joint key with your right little finger.

The Note Upper C

9. Upper C Exercises

Here are some exercises you can use to practice playing the note Upper C.

Upper C, half notes, exercise 1

Upper C, quarter notes, exercise 1

Upper C, whole notes, exercise 1

Upper C, eighth notes, exercise 1

Upper C, half notes, exercise 2

Upper C, quarter notes, exercise 2

Upper C, whole notes, exercise 2

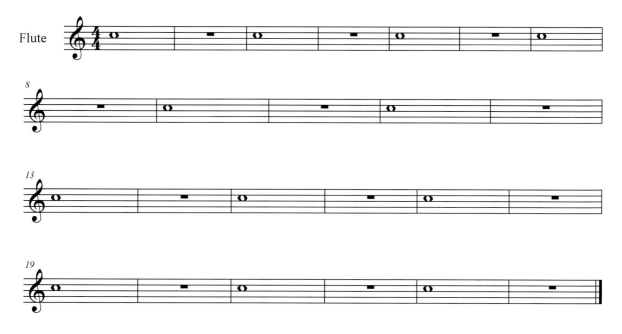

Upper C, eighth notes, exercise 2

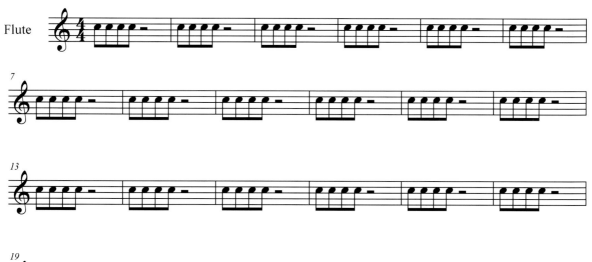

10. Practicing What You Know: F Through Upper C

Now that you've mastered the Upper C, you're ready to practice playing it with the other notes that you've learned. In the following lessons, you'll play the notes on the scale between F and the Upper C. Watch the key signature; some of these exercises are in the key of F, so you play Bb instead of B.

The Notes F through Upper C, half notes, exercise 1

Watch the "accidental" flat sign in measures four, seven, and fourteen.

The Notes F through Upper C, quarter notes, exercise 1

The Notes F through Upper C, whole notes, exercise 1

The Notes F through Upper C, eighth notes, exercise 1

The Notes F through Upper C, half notes, exercise 2

The Notes F through Upper C, quarter notes, exercise 2

The Notes F through Upper C, whole notes, exercise 2

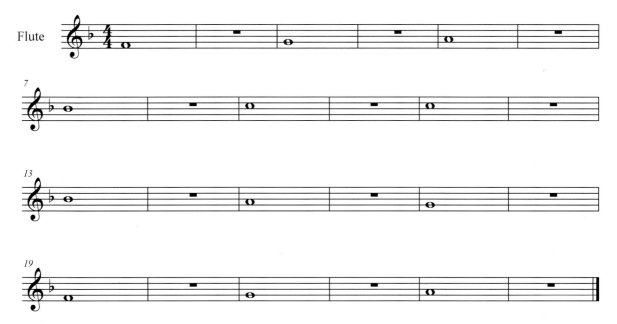

The Notes F through Upper C, eighth notes, exercise 2

Young flute players in Cork, Ireland, circa 1905.

11. The Note Upper D

To play this note, close the keys underneath your left thumb and the second and third keys with your middle and ring fingers. Close the first, second, and third keys with your right index, middle, and ring finger. Do not close the foot joint key.

The Note Upper D

12. Upper D Exercises

Here are some exercises you can use to practice playing the note Upper D.

Upper D, half notes, exercise 1

Upper D, quarter notes, exercise 1

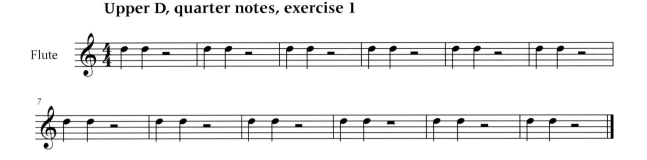

Upper D, whole notes, exercise 1

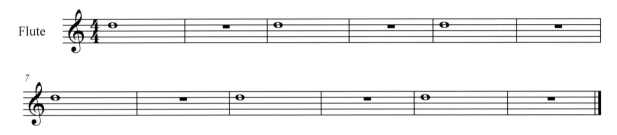

Upper D, eighth notes, exercise 1

Upper D, half notes, exercise 2

Upper D, quarter notes, exercise 2

Upper D, whole notes, exercise 2

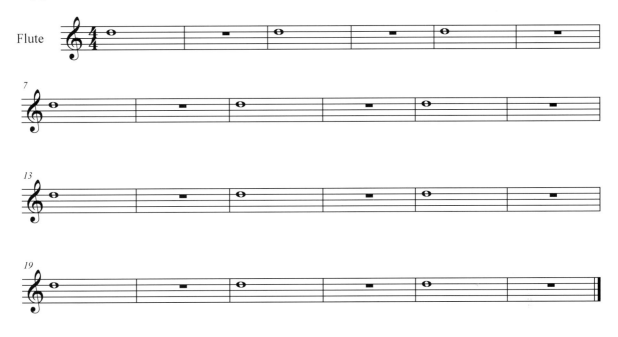

Upper D, eighth notes, exercise 2

13. The Note Upper Eb

Close the keys underneath your left thumb and the second and third keys with your left middle and ring fingers. Close the first, second, and third keys on your right hand, as well as the foot joint key with your right little finger.

The Note Upper Eb

14. Upper Eb Exercises

Here are some exercises you can use to practice playing the note Upper Eb.

Upper Eb, half notes, exercise 1

Upper Eb, quarter notes, exercise 1

Upper Eb, whole notes, exercise 1

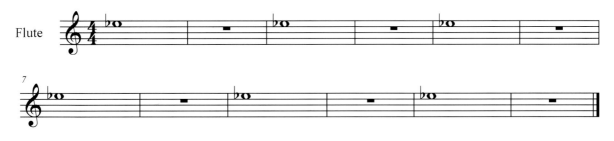

Upper Eb, eighth notes, exercise 1

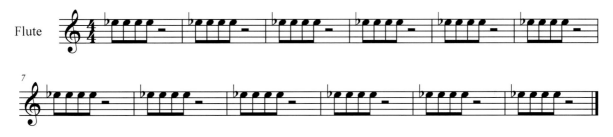

Upper Eb, half notes, exercise 2

Upper Eb, quarter notes, exercise 2

Upper Eb, whole notes, exercise 2

Upper Eb, eighth notes, exercise 2

15. The Note Upper E

For the Upper E, close the keys underneath your left thumb and the first, second, and third keys with your index, middle, and ring fingers. On the right hand, close the first and second keys with your index and middle fingers and the foot joint key with your right little finger.

The Note Upper E

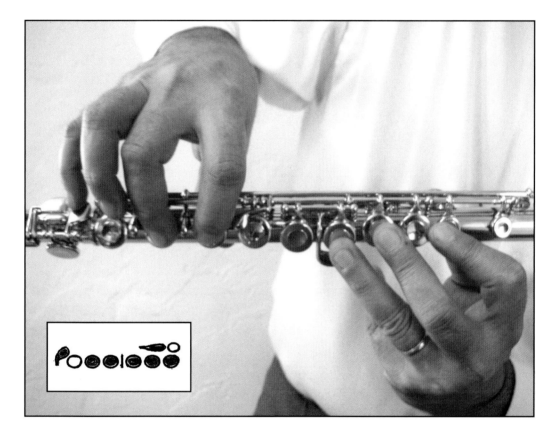

16. Upper E Exercises

Here are some exercises you can use to practice playing the Upper E. At the end of the section are three well-known songs. You're ready to play them using the notes you've learned.

Upper E, half notes, exercise 1

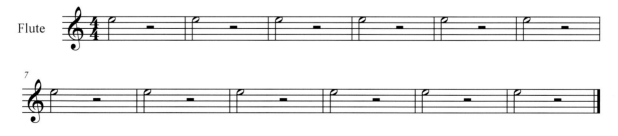

Upper E, quarter notes, exercise 1

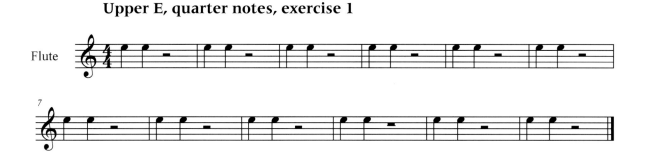

Upper E, whole notes, exercise 1

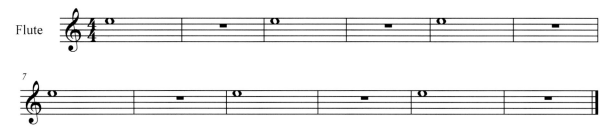

Upper E, eighth notes, exercise 1

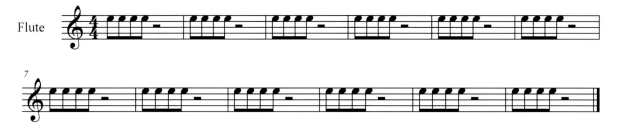

Upper E, half notes, exercise 2

Upper E, quarter notes, exercise 2

Upper E, whole notes, exercise 2

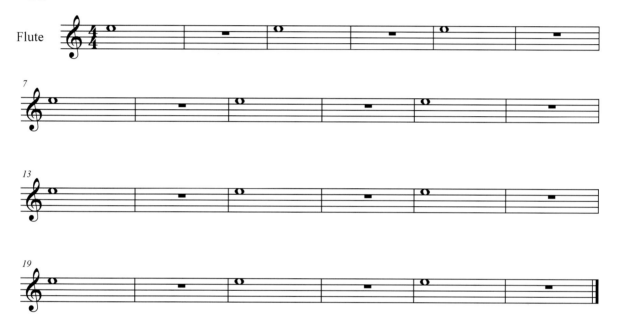

Upper E, eighth notes, exercise 2

Old Dan Tucker

Dan Emmett

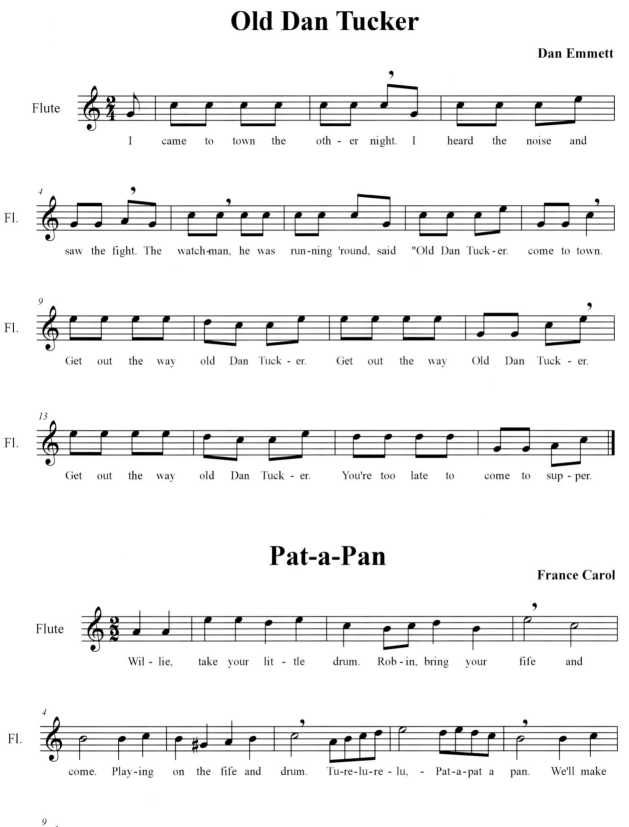

Flute

I came to town the oth - er night. I heard the noise and

Fl.

saw the fight. The watch-man, he was run-ning 'round, said "Old Dan Tuck - er. come to town.

Fl.

Get out the way old Dan Tuck - er. Get out the way Old Dan Tuck - er.

Fl.

Get out the way old Dan Tuck - er. You're too late to come to sup - per.

Pat-a-Pan

France Carol

Flute

Wil - lie, take your lit - tle drum. Rob - in, bring your fife and

Fl.

come. Play-ing on the fife and drum. Tu-re-lu-re-lu, - Pat-a-pat a pan. We'll make

Fl.

mu - sic loud and gay for our Christ - mas hol - i - day.

Old MacDonald Had a Farm

American

Old Mac - Don - ald had a farm, E I E I O. And

on his farm he had some ducks, E I E I O. With a

quack, quack, here, and a quack, quack, there. Here a quack. There a quack. Eve-ry where a quack, quack.

Old Mac - Don - ald had a farm, E I E I O.

17. The Note Upper F

To play the Upper F, use the same fingering that you used to play the lower F. Close the keys underneath your left thumb and the three fingers of your left hand. Close the keys underneath the first finger of your right hand and the first key on the foot joint with your right little finger. The other fingers should rest in their positions and not press any keys. To play the higher note, you must blow a little harder and purse your lips more than you would if playing the lower F.

The Note Upper F

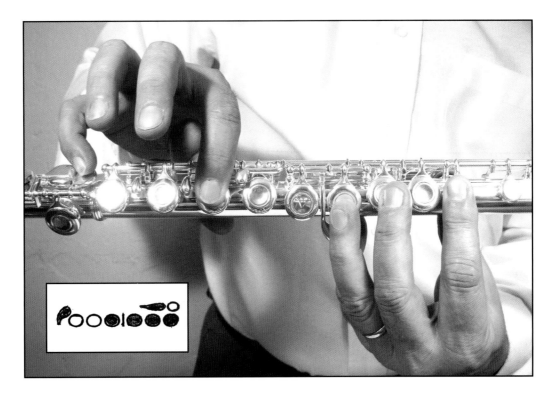

18. Upper F Exercises

Here are some exercises you can use to practice playing the note Upper F.

Upper F, half notes, exercise 1

Flute

Upper F, quarter notes, exercise 1

Upper F, whole notes, exercise 1

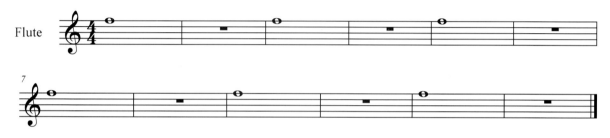

Upper F, eighth notes, exercise 1

Upper F, half notes, exercise 2

Upper F, quarter notes, exercise 2

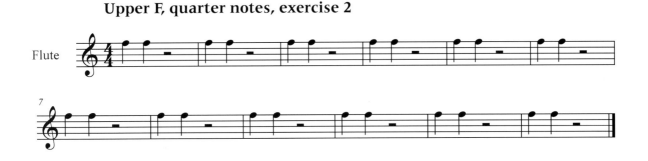

Upper F, whole notes, exercise 2

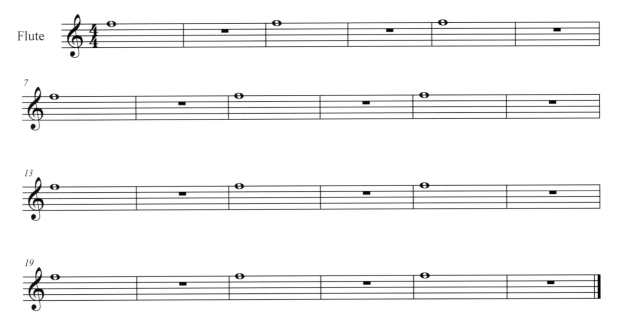

Upper F, eighth notes, exercise 2

19. F Scales and New Songs

Now that you have mastered the notes F through Upper F, you will be able to play scales. Here is the F scale, followed by a number of songs you should be able to play. Both scales are the same—one has the flat in the key signature, and the other shows it in the music. If you know the song "Do, Re, Mi," these scales will sound familiar when you play them.

The F scale, half notes in the key of F

The F scale, half notes in the key of C

Flutes Up

Bingo

Scotland

There was a farm-er had a dog, and Bin-go was his name O. B I N G O B I N G O B I N G O and Bin go was his name O.

Jacob's Ladder

Spiritual

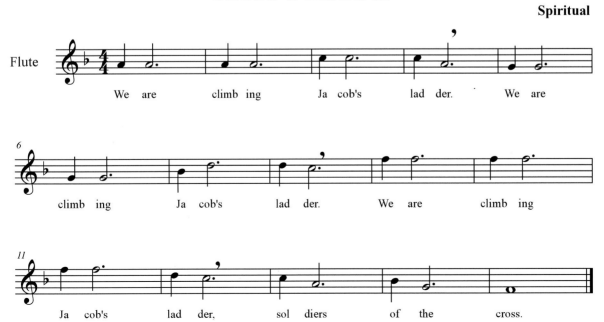

We are climb ing Ja cob's lad der. We are climb ing Ja cob's lad der. We are climb ing Ja cob's lad der, sol diers of the cross.

Aura Lee

American

As the black-bird in the spring 'neath the wil-low tree

sat and piped, I heard him sing, sing-ing Au - ra Lee.

Au - ra Lee, Au - ra Lee, maid of gold - en hair,

sun - shine came a - long with thee and swal - lows in the air.

On Top of Old Smokey

American folk song

On top of old Smo key all cov ered with snow,____

__ I lost my true lov er by court in' too slow.

Camptown Races

Stephen Foster

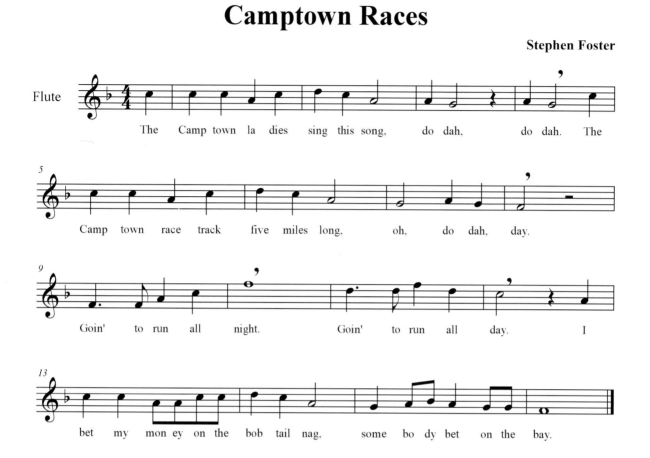

The Camp town la dies sing this song, do dah, do dah. The

Camp town race track five miles long, oh, do dah, day.

Goin' to run all night. Goin' to run all day. I

bet my mon ey on the bob tail nag, some bo dy bet on the bay.

Flutes Today

Lullaby

World Folk Song

Sleep, my ba - by on my bos - om, warm and cos - y will it prove.

Round thee moth - er's arms are foldi - ing, in her heart a moth - er's love.

There shall no one come to harm thee. Naught shall ev - er break thy rest.

Sleep, my ba - by on my bos - om, warm and cos - y will it prove.

Toot Your Flute

20. The Note Upper G

For this note, close the keys underneath your left thumb and the three fingers on your left hand. Close only the key on the foot joint with your right little finger. To play the higher note, you must blow a little harder and purse your lips more than you would if playing the lower G.

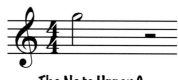

The Note Upper G

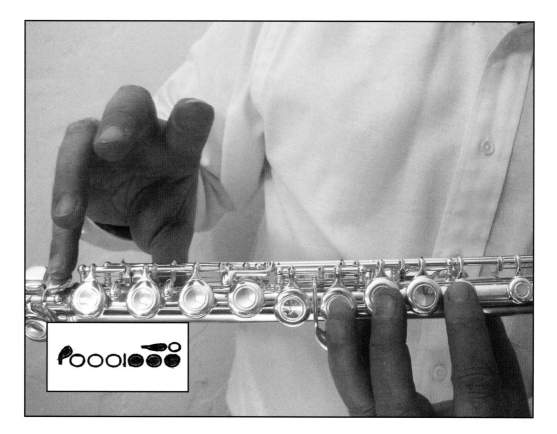

21. Upper G Exercises

Here are some exercises you can use to practice playing the Upper G.

Upper G, half notes, exercise 1

Upper G, quarter notes, exercise 1

Upper G, whole notes, exercise 1

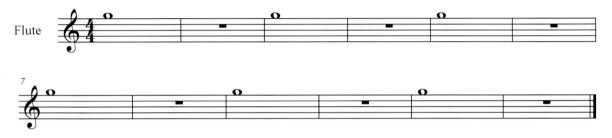

Upper G, eighth notes, exercise 1

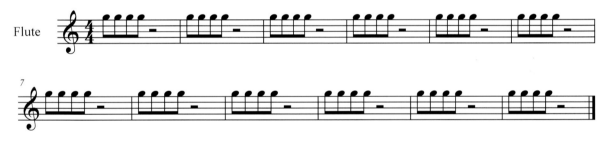

Upper G, half notes, exercise 2

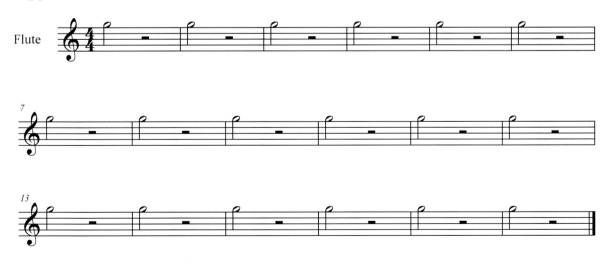

Upper G, quarter notes, exercise 2

Upper G, whole notes, exercise 2

Upper G, eighth notes, exercise 2

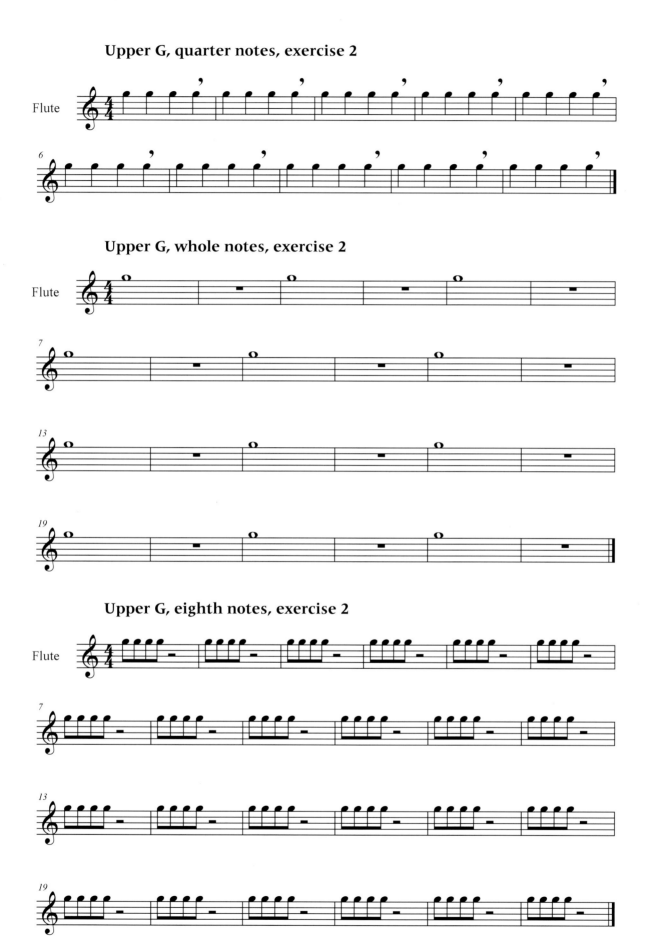

Polly Wolly Doodle

American

Did You Ever See a Lassie

Germany

Did you ev er see a lass ie, a las sie, a las sie? Did you

ev er see a las sie go this way and that? Go this way and that way and

that way and that way. Did you ev er see a las sie go this way and that?

Down in the Valley

American Folk

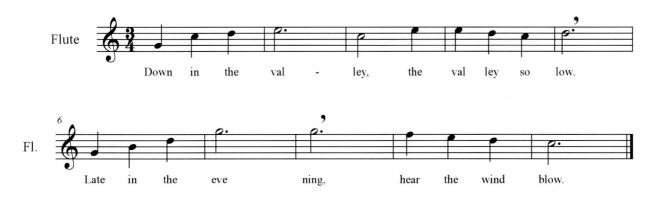

Down in the val - ley, the val ley so low.

Late in the eve ning, hear the wind blow.

22. The Note Upper A

Close the keys underneath your left thumb and the first and second fingers on your left hand. Close only the key on the foot joint with your right little finger. To play the higher note, you must blow a little harder and purse your lips more than you would if playing the lower A.

The Note Upper A

23. Upper A Exercises

Here are some exercises you can use to practice playing the Upper A.

Upper A, half notes, exercise 1

Upper A, quarter notes, exercise 1

Upper A, whole notes, exercise 1

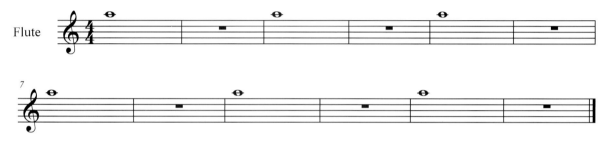

Upper A, eighth notes, exercise 1

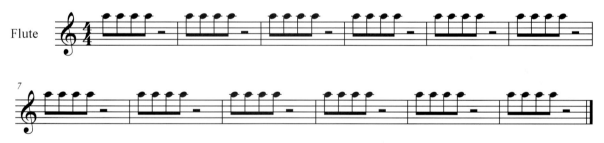

Upper A, half notes, exercise 2

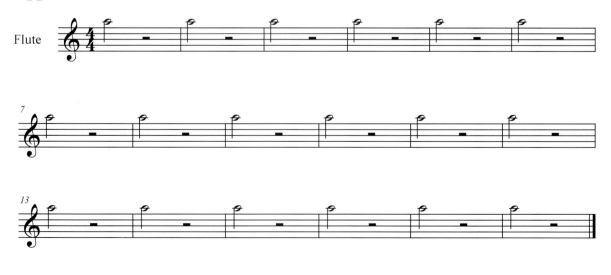

Upper A, quarter notes, exercise 2

Upper A, whole notes, exercise 2

Upper A, eighth notes, exercise 2

24. The F Scale

Here are some scales to play to review the notes that you have learned.

F scale, quarter notes

Flute

F scale, half notes

Flute

Fl.
5

F scale, half notes and half rests, up and down

Flute

Fl.
5

Fl.
9

Fl.
13

25. The Note E

With this next note, you will be able to add a few more songs to your repertoire. To play the E, close the keys underneath your left thumb and the first, second, and third keys with your index, middle, and ring fingers. Close the first and sec-ond keys with your right index and middle fingers. Close the foot joint key with your right little finger.

The Note E

26. E Exercises

Here are some exercises you can use to practice playing the note E.

E, half notes, exercise 1

E, quarter notes, exercise 1

E, whole notes, exercise 1

E, eighth notes, exercise 1

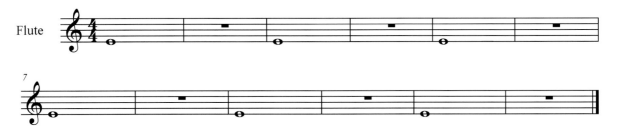

E, half notes, exercise 2

E, quarter notes, exercise 2

E, whole notes, exercise 2

E, eighth notes, exercise 2

27. Playing the Notes You Know

Here are some exercises you can use to practice playing the notes E, F, and G. At the end of this section are some popular songs that use most of the notes you've learned to this point.

E and F, half notes, exercise 1

E and F, quarter notes, exercise 1

E and F, whole notes, exercise 1

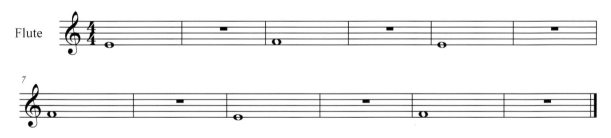

E and F, eighth notes, exercise 1

E and F, half notes, exercise 2

E and F, quarter notes, exercise 2

E and F, whole notes, exercise 2

E and F, eighth notes, exercise 2

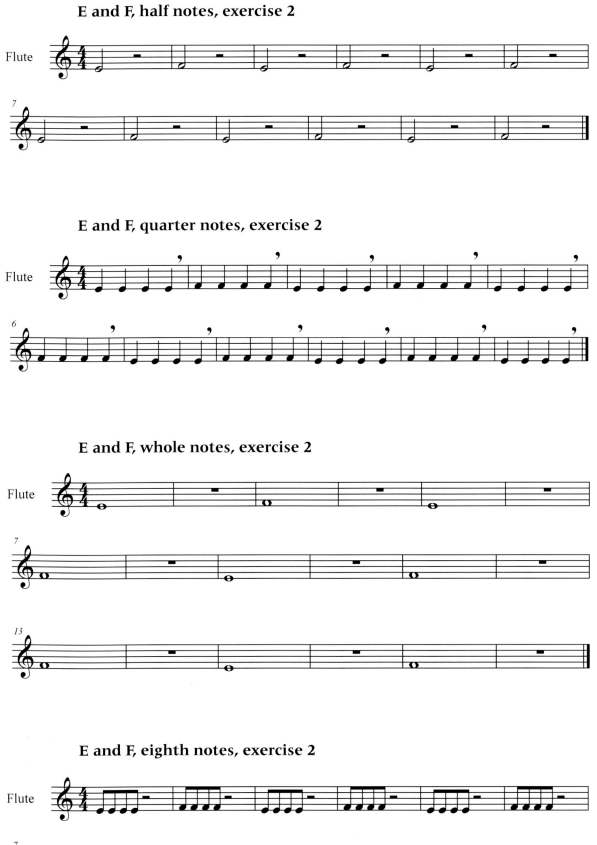

E, F, and G, half notes, exercise 1

E, F, and G, half notes, exercise 2

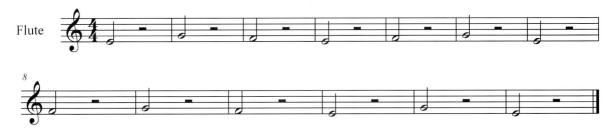

E, F, and G, quarter notes, exercise 1

E, F, and G, quarter notes, exercise 2

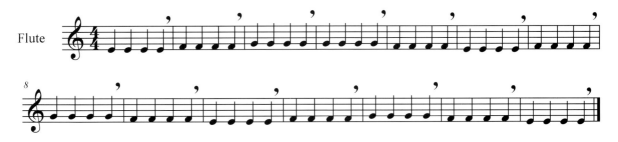

E, F, and G, quarter notes, exercise 3

My Bonnie

England

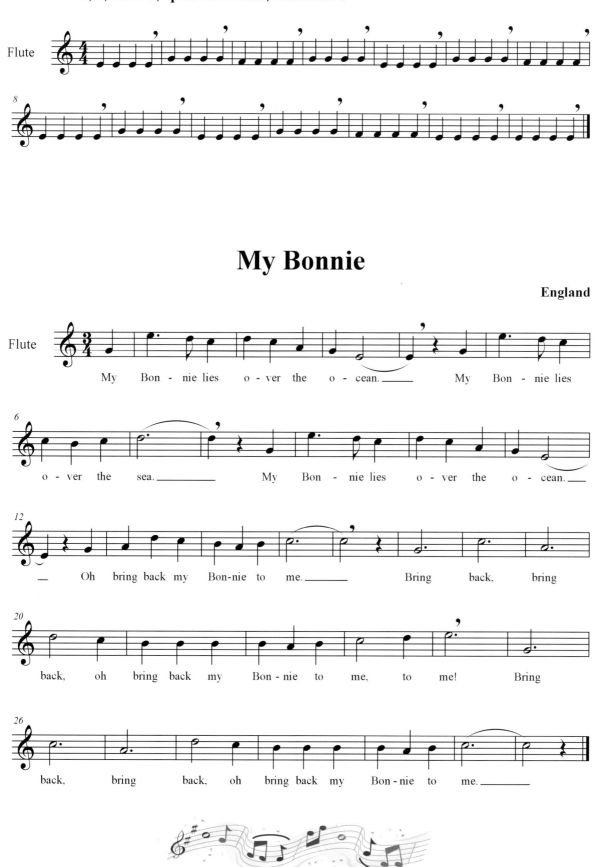

He's Got the Whole World in His Hands

Spiritual

Flute

He's got the whole wor ld in his hands. He's got the

whole wor ld in his hands. He's got the whole wor ld

in his hands. He's got the whole world in his hands.

28. The Note Upper B

Now let's try playing the Upper B. Close the keys underneath your left thumb and the first key with your index finger on your left hand. Also close the foot joint key with your right little finger. To play the higher note, you must blow a lit-

The Note Upper B

tle harder and purse your lips more than you would if playing the lower B.

29. Upper B Exercises

Here are some exercises you can use to practice playing the Upper B.

Upper B, half notes, exercise 1

Upper B, quarter notes, exercise 1

Upper B, whole notes, exercise 1

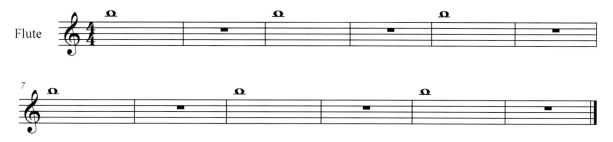

Upper B, eighth notes, exercise 1

Upper B, half notes, exercise 2

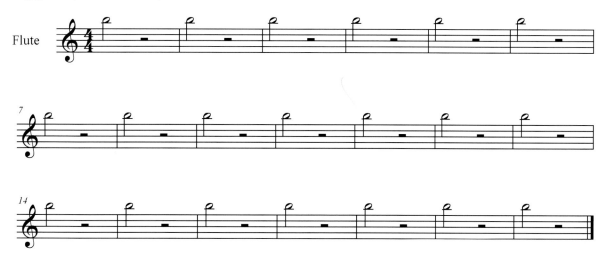

Upper B, quarter notes, exercise 2

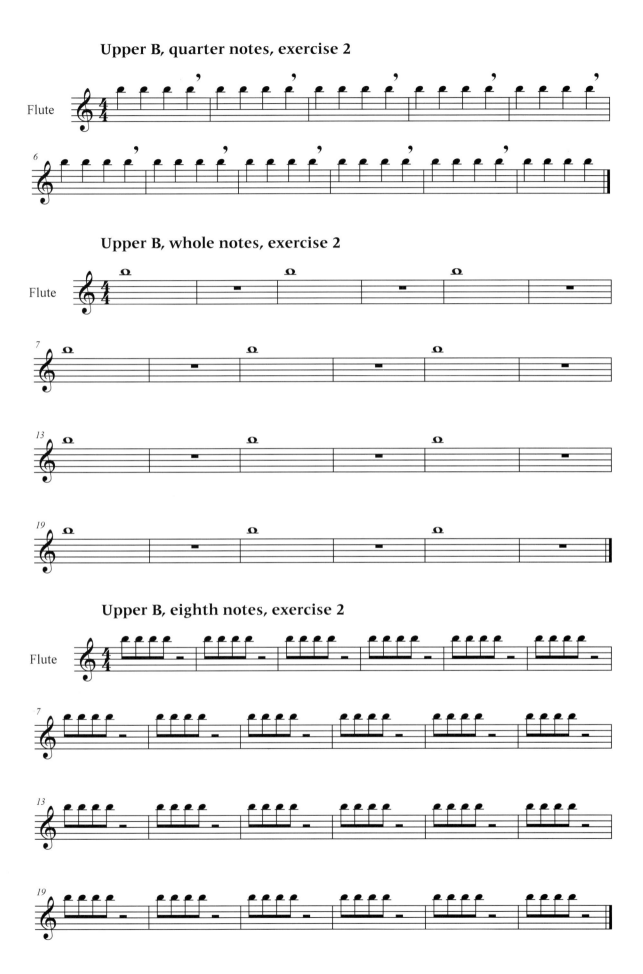

Upper B, whole notes, exercise 2

Upper B, eighth notes, exercise 2

30. The Note High C

Close only the first key with the index finger of your left hand and the foot joint key with your right little finger. To play the higher note, you must blow a little harder and purse your lips more than you would if playing the lower C.

The Note High C

31. High C Exercises

Here are some exercises you can use to practice playing the High C.

High C, half notes, exercise 1

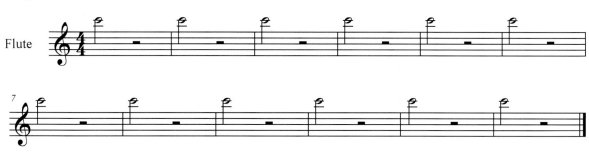

High C, quarter notes, exercise 1

High C, whole notes, exercise 1

High C, eighth notes, exercise 1

High C, half notes, exercise 2

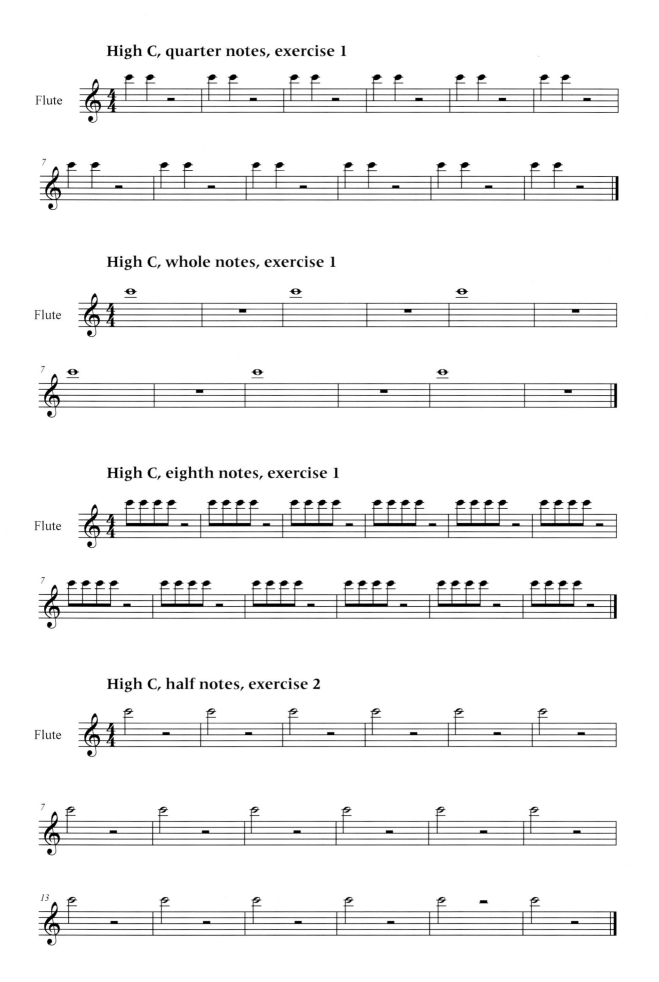

High C, quarter notes, exercise 2

High C, whole notes, exercise 2

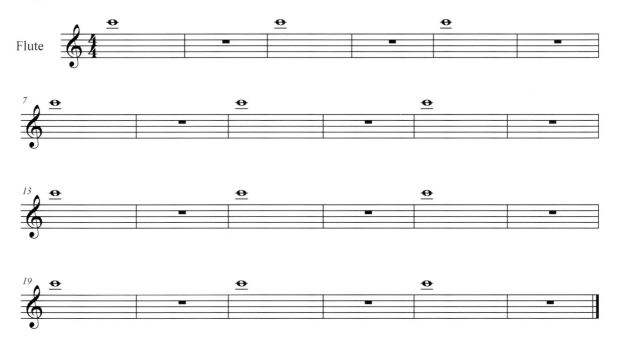

High C, eighth notes, exercise 2

Little Brown Jug

Traditional

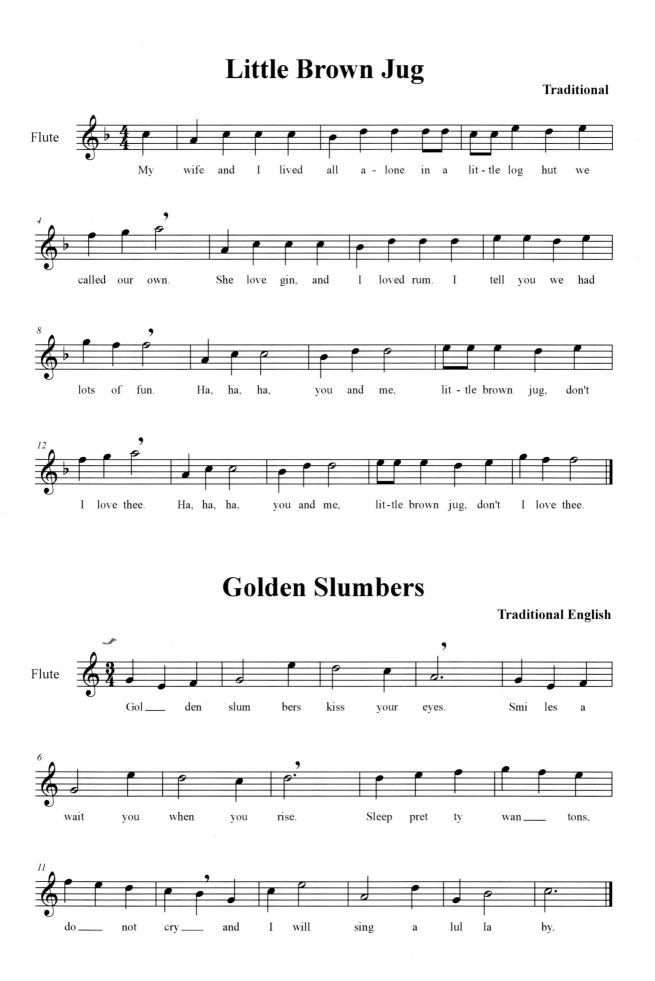

My wife and I lived all a-lone in a lit-tle log hut we

called our own.   She love gin, and I loved rum.   I tell you we had

lots of fun.   Ha, ha, ha,   you and me,   lit-tle brown jug, don't

I love thee.   Ha, ha, ha,   you and me,   lit-tle brown jug, don't I love thee.

Golden Slumbers

Traditional English

Gol__ den slum bers kiss your eyes.   Smi les a

wait you when you rise.   Sleep pret ty wan__ tons,

do__ not cry__ and I will   sing a lul la by.

Good King Wenceslas

Traditional European

Good King Wen ces las looked out on the feast of Ste phen,

when the snow lay round a bout, deep and crisp, and e ven.

Bright ly shone the moon that night, though the frost was cru el,

when a poor man came in sight, gath ring win ter fu el.

HELPFUL TIP:
The higher the note, the more difficult it will be to play with a pleasing sound. Keep practicing the high notes until you can produce a clear tone.

APPENDIX: Finding the Notes

Regardless of which instrument a student of music is learning, a diagram of the keys of the piano offers one of the best illustrations of how most western music is organized. Comprehending the relationship between different notes gives a flutist both a greater understanding of his or her instrument and a grasp of the basics of music theory.

Typically, a modern piano has around 88 keys. As you can see in the diagram on the opposite page, these keys are colored either black or white and repeat a specific pattern throughout the keyboard. That is, with the exception of the extreme left of the keyboard (the lowest notes) and the extreme right (the highest notes), you will find groupings of three white keys with two black keys between them and four white keys with three black keys between them. Each of these keys is given a name corresponding to the letters of the alphabet A through G. The letter names are assigned to the white, and the black keys' names are letters with either a sharp sign or flat sign after them.

The pitch that sounds when you strike the white key immediately to the left of the grouping of two black keys is known as C. Depending upon the number of keys on the piano being played, this note will reoccur six or seven times throughout the instrument. The frequency of each C is twice that of the C immediately to its left and one-half that of the C to its right. Because of this special relationship, these notes sound very similar to our ears, hence, the reason why they have the same name. The interval between these adjacent pitches with the same name is known as an octave, and this relationship is true for all similarly named notes found on the keyboard.

In order to clear up confusion caused by the fact that there are as many as 88 notes (maybe more) on a piano and many fewer note names, musicians, over time, have developed a way to differentiate between the notes that have the same name. Beginning with the C note found farthest to the left of the keyboard, a number is added to the note name indicating the octave in which the note occurs. For example, the first C that appears on the

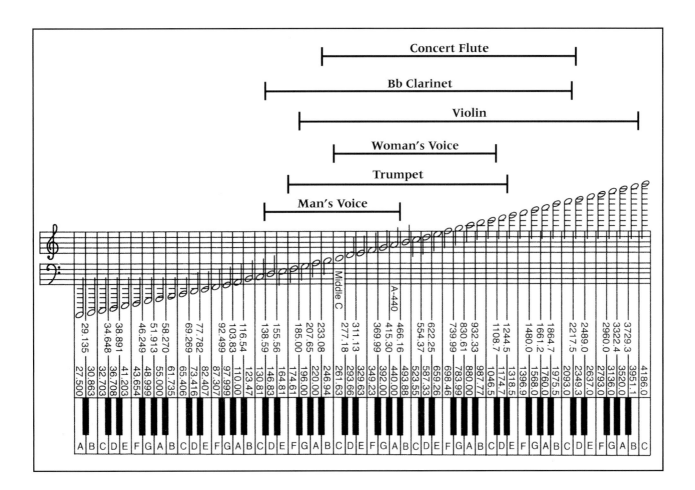

keyboard is known as "C1," the D that appears next to that is known as "D1," and so on. Middle C is also known as C4. Depending upon the piano's manufacturer, you may find that there is a different number of notes to the left of the first C on the keyboard. Since these notes do not comprise a complete octave, the number zero follows their letter name.

You'll notice that there are eleven keys between notes of the same name. Each of these keys represents a change in pitch of one half step. It can then be concluded that an octave covers a distance of 12 half steps, or six whole steps.

FLUTE TIMELINE

30,000 B.C: A flute carved from a mammoth tusk was dated to this era.

A.D. 900: The earliest depictions of a transverse flute in Western culture appear in Byzantine art.

ca. 1320: A flute two feet long in the key of D is made.

1670: Flutes begin appearing in French and German opera and chamber music in the 1680s. Jean-Baptiste Lully's opera-ballet *Le Triomphe de l'Amour* (1681) first specifies "Flûtes d'Allemagne," or German flutes, another term for the traverse flute.

1702: The flute begins gaining popularity as a solo instrument. Michel de Labarre's *Pieces pour la flûte traversière avec la basse-continue* is one of the first collections of flute music to be published.

1722: Flutist Johann Joachim Quantz alters his flute, adding the C# key on the foot joint and a tuning cork to the head joint.

1726: Quantz adds the Eb and D# keys to the foot joint. Michel Blavet enjoys a success as a soloist in Paris.

1752: Quantz's *Essay on a Method of Playing the Transverse Flute*, a mammoth treatise on flute playing, is published in German and French.

1760: The G#, Bb, and F keys are added to the flute by the London instrument makers Florio, Gedney, and Potter.

ca. 1790: Four-keyed flutes are used by Mozart and Haydn.

ca. 1800: Beethoven adds flutes to his symphonies.

1810: Flutes begin to be made out of metal.

1821: Eight-keyed flutes are invented.

1826: Theobald Boehm gives up his goldsmith's business to pursue a career in flute performance and opens a flute-making workshop.

1832: Boehm adds open holes to his flute, employing ring keys that cover and uncover additional holes when the standard keys are played.

1846: Boehm decides to make his flutes out of silver while adding more holes and keys.

1860: The influential Conservatoire de Paris adopts Boehm flutes, effectively ensuring that Boehm's design will become the standard for Western music.

1888: William S. Haynes and his brother George begin making Boehm flutes in Boston.

1890-1910: Recordings of flute players become more common. A female flutist in Germany records in 1906. (However, women are still excluded from most orchestral positions until after the Second World War.)

1925: Electric microphones, "high fidelity" recording, and radio encourages a few flutists to record extensively.

1932: Wayman Carver of the Chick Webb Band becomes the first well-known jazz flute specialist.

1948: Alexander Murray develops a flute with a corrected C# key.

1950: Magnetic tape and long-playing records begin a boom in the recording industry. Jean-Pierre Rampal begins his recording career with a vast quantity of unknown baroque music.

Late 1960s: Various alto and bass flutes are invented for use in modern music and in flute ensembles. Composers begin to use electronics and percussion more in combination with the flute.

ca. 1990: Boehm flutes are no longer used by mainstream professional flutists, who now nearly all play the same "French model" flute.

2006: In recognition of his lifelong contribution to popular music, flutist Ian Anderson of the rock band Jethro Tull receives two honors: the Ivor Novello Award for International Achievement and an honorary Doctorate of Literature from Heriot-Watt University.

INTERNET RESOURCES

http://www.menc.org/

The mission of the National Association for Music Education is to "advance music education by encouraging the study and making of music by all." Go to this site for more information and articles related to issues in music education, making a donation, and how you can become a member.

http://musiced.about.com/od/beginnersguide/bb/bflute.htm

At this website you'll find a list of helpful tips for buying your first flute.

http://www.8notes.com/

A great resource for all musicians, this site has flute sheet music for 55 songs available for free download, along with fingering charts, a glossary of music terms, a free online metronome, and links to other useful music websites.

http://www.ibreathemusic.com/

An invaluable resource for any musician, this site has forums and articles covering a wide range of music-related topics, including composition, improvisation, and ear training.

http://www.zacharymusic.com/Zachary_Music/FLcarePics.htm

Here you'll find a highly informative article describing, in detail, how to care for your flute. High quality color photos illustrate each step of the process.

http://www.fluteland.com/

This website has online lessons, ways to find your own flute teacher, and a forum for flute-related topics, among many other valuable resources for flute enthusiasts.

http://www.jazzreview.com/

An excellent website for everything associated with jazz. Here you'll find CD and concert reviews, interviews with numerous musicians, and dozens of jazz-related articles.

GLOSSARY

Accidental—a sharp, flat, or natural note that occurs in a piece of music but is not indicated in the key signature.

Bar lines—these vertical lines mark the division between measures of music.

Beat—the pulse of the music, which is usually implied using the combination of accented and unaccented notes throughout the composition.

Chord—three or more different tones played at the same time.

Clef (bass and treble)—located on the left side of each line of music, these symbols indicate the names and pitch of the notes corresponding to their lines and spaces.

Eighth note—a note with a solid oval, a stem, and a single tail that has 1/8 the value of a whole note.

Embouchure—the adjustment of the lips and tongue in playing a woodwind instrument.

Enharmonic notes—notes that are written differently in a musical score, but have the same pitch when played (for example, F# and Gb).

Flat sign (b)—a symbol that indicates that the note following it should be lowered by one half step. This remains in effect for an entire measure, unless otherwise indicated by a natural sign.

Half note—a note with a hollow oval and stem that has 1/2 the value of a whole note.

Half step—a unit of measurement in music that is the smallest distance between two notes, either ascending or descending. An octave is divided equally into 12 half steps.

Interval—the distance in pitch between two tones, indicated using half and whole steps.

Key signature—found between the clef and time signature, it describes which notes to play with sharps or flats throughout a piece of music.

Measure—a unit of music contained between two adjacent bar lines.

Music staff—the horizontal lines and spaces between and upon which music is written.

Natural sign—a symbol which instructs that a note should not be played as a sharp or a flat.

Notes—written or printed symbols which represent the frequency and duration of tones contained in a piece of music.

Octave—a relationship between two pitches where one tone has double (or half) the frequency of the other.

Pitch—the perceived highness or lowness of a sound or tone.

Quarter note—a note with a solid oval and a stem that is played for 1/4 of the duration of a whole note.

Repeat sign—a pair of vertical dots that appear near bar lines that indicate a section of music that is to be played more than once.

Rest—a figure that is used to denote silence for a given duration in a piece of music.

Scale—a sequence of notes in order of pitch in ascending or descending order.

Sharp sign (#)—this symbol indicates that the note following it should be raised by one half-step. This remains in effect for an entire measure, unless otherwise indicated by a natural sign.

Tempo—the speed at which music is to be played. It is notated by either a word describing the relative speed of the piece or by the number of beats per minute (B.P.M.) that occur as it is played.

Time signature—located to the right of the clef and key signatures, the top digit indicates the number of beats per measure, and the number at the bottom shows which kind of note receives one beat.

Tone—a distinct musical sound which can be produced by a voice or instrument.

Whole note—a note indicated by a hollow oval without a stem. It has the longest time value and represents a length of 4 beats when written in 4/4 time.

Whole step—a unit of measurement in music that is equal to two half steps.

INDEX

"Aura Lee," 73

"Bingo," 72
Boehm, 9
Breathing, 24
Breathing marks, 23

"Camptown Races," 74
cleaning, 15
clef
    bass, 20
    treble, 20

"Did You Ever See a Lassie," 80
"Down in the Valley," 80

F scales, 71, 85
fife, 9
flute
    assembling, 12
    body joint, 13
    buying, 10–11
    foot joint, 13
    head joint, 13
    history, 9, 104–105
    holding, 25–27
    making a sound, 24–25
    renting, 11
"Flutes Today," 74

"Golden Slumbers," 100
"Good King Wenceslas," 101

"He's Got the Whole World in His
    Hands," 93

"Jacob's Ladder," 72

"Little Brown Jug," 100
"Lullaby," 75

music
    clef, 20
    reading, 16–23
    staff, 16
    time signature, 20–21
"My Bonnie," 92

notes
    A, 40–44, 54–56
    B, 48–50, 54–56
    Bb, 45–47, 54–56
    dotted, 18
    E, 86–92
    eighth, 18
    F, 29–32, 36–39, 43–44
    flats, 21–22
    G, 33–39, 43–44, 54–56
    half, 18
    High C, 97–99
    quarter, 18
    reading, 19
    rests, 18
    sharps, 21–22
    Upper A, 82–84
    Upper B, 94–96
    Upper C, 51–56
    Upper D, 57–59
    Upper E, 63–65
    Upper Eb, 60–62
    Upper F, 68–70
    Upper G, 76–78
    whole, 18

"Old Dan Tucker," 66
"Old MacDonald Had a Farm," 67
"On Top of Old Smokey," 73

"Pat-a-Pan," 66
"Polly Wolly Doodle," 79

time signature, 20–21
"Toot Your Flute," 75

ABOUT THE AUTHOR

Frank Cappelli is a warm, engaging artist, who possesses the special ability to transform the simple things of life into a wonderful musical experience. He has had an impressive career since receiving a B.A. in music education from West Chester State College (now West Chester University). Frank has performed his music at many American venues—from Disney World in Florida to Knott's Berry Farm in California—as well as in Ireland, Spain, France, and Italy. He has also performed with the Detroit Symphony, the Buffalo Philharmonic, the Pittsburgh Symphony, and the Chattanooga Symphony.

In 1987, Frank created Peanut Heaven, a record label for children. The following year, he worked with WTAE-TV in Pittsburgh to develop *Cappelli and Company*, an award winning children's television variety show. The weekly program premiered in 1989, and is now internationally syndicated.

In 1989, Frank signed a contract with A&M Records, which released his four albums for children (*Look Both Ways, You Wanna Be a Duck?, On Vacation,* and *Good*) later that year. *Pass the Coconut* was released by A&M in 1991. *Take a Seat* was released in September of 1993. With the 1990 A&M Video release of *All Aboard the Train and Other Favorites* and *Slap Me Five*, Cappelli's popular television program first became available to kids nationwide. Both videos have received high marks from a number of national publications, including *People Magazine, Video Insider, Billboard, USA Today, Entertainment Weekly,* and *TV Guide*.

Frank has received many awards, including the Parent's Choice Gold Award, regional Emmy Awards, the Gabriel Award for Outstanding Achievement in Children's Programming, and the Achievement in Children's Television Award. He is a three-time recipient of the Pennsylvania Association of Broadcasters' award for Best Children's Program in Pennsylvania.